I0112145

AFFIRMATIONS FOR ENTREPRENEURS

DAILY MANTRAS FOR LIFE, LOVE, AND LIBERTY

GAFAR LIAMEED

ROYALVIEWZ WORTHY GROUP LLC

Copyright © 2023 by Gafar Liameed

www.royalviewz.com

All rights reserved.

No portion of this book may be reproduced, distributed, or transmitted in any form or by any means, including photocopying, recording, or other electronic or mechanical methods, without the prior written permission of the publisher and author, except in the case of brief quotations embodied in critical reviews and certain other noncommercial uses permitted by copyright law. For permission requests, write to the author, addressed "Attention: Permissions" at royalviewz.mgmt@gmail.com.

Printed in the United States of America

ISBN: 979-8-9877905-0-2

To the wise server who chooses to impact the world and its people. Be courageous and never lose faith. Be open-minded and never stop learning. You are capable and blessed within.

INTRODUCTION

As an independent thinker and creative professional, I've always been driven to make my mark on the world. Born in Brooklyn in 1994, raised in Lagos, and now living in Chicago, I've been on a journey to find my place in this wicked world. And while I've faced my share of pain, I've always stayed humble and true to my beliefs.

I've learned the power of emotional intelligence and the importance of economic trade and education in the arts. That's why I wrote "Affirmations for Entrepreneurs," a devotional guide and reference book for budding and established creative professionals who seek a new positive belief system to aid concentration in meditation and practice of their craft and trade. With this book, I hope to liberate the idea of the starving artist and empower artists to achieve economic success while staying true to their art.

As The Gentle Spokesperson, I've also made it my mission to spread positivity and inspire others to achieve their goals. I've dedicated my life to becoming a Nigerian and American classic for the next 20-30 years. Affirmations for Entrepreneurs is a timeless piece of literature that will inspire millions of readers to take control of their lives and achieve greatness.

So if you're an entrepreneur, artist, or just someone looking for inspiration, I invite you to join me on this journey of self-discovery and empowerment. Together, we can achieve anything we set our minds to.

THE MANTRA

In all things desired, get started!

I AFFIRM

In pursuit of my goals and dreams, everything between now and a lifetime of experiences is mere noise. I will cherish the moments filled with positive lessons and meaningful experiences, and reflect on them, rather than dwell on constant failures and negativity.

MAKE ROOM

I am "me" first, before my potential. It is everything I do today that creates the potential that is tomorrow.

NO WAY AROUND

There's no way around the work I must do to become successful. Drilling that concept into my being is what will make me great.

PURPOSE-DRIVEN

I choose to be accountable because my livelihood depends on it.

HONORABLE SELF

Controlling the narrative means to
honor the way you represent yourself,
your mission, your message, and your
purpose in any circumstance of life, love,
and liberty.

ACCOUNTABILITY

There's a certain peace in having no one to blame but myself. Recognizing the results of my own actions leads to my growth, development, and self-understanding, or to my denial. I won't live in denial. I'll continue to make things happen for myself and those I love.

URGENCY

Time doesn't wait for your mood or feelings to adjust. While everything happens for a reason, you'd do well to ensure that you are making things happen.

SHOOTING STAR

It won't be what I'm looking for until it is. My time. My effort. My results. I must show up for myself. I must take charge of the results I expect. I must! It's foolish to believe that I can expect from others what I haven't already dedicated time to learning myself. I must know the ins and outs of my vision to complete it.

NO EXCUSES

My lack of effort to show up for an opportunity can't be my excuse for depression.

HARD TRUTH

The reason you think you can't do it is because you haven't started. The truth about change is that it's what you make it.

HARSH TRUTH

Lessons come fast from all aspects of life. I reflect on myself and adjust accordingly. I accept what is and put aside what isn't. There's peace in accountability, so I'll avoid raging thoughts of procrastination. I must do better once I've learned better.

THE DEAL

There's always going to be something and nothing you don't like. Don't get flustered by the idea of perfection. Starting something happens to be more progressive than doing nothing at all.

GOD FIRST

When everyone else disappoints and proves to be unavailable, remember that you should've turned to God and yourself first. The results will always be consistent.

LUXURIES

Encouragement and support are two different luxuries that often come when it matters most.

SMALL TALK

Say less and do more. Create an action plan and adjust while in process.

LISTEN WELL

Attention is easy to gain but hard to maintain. There's plenty of value in being a good listener and observer. Articulate your ideas with passion, empathy, and purpose.

THRIVE

I refuse to be content with living in survival mode.

SERIOUSLY CONSIDERED

People are fickle at first glance. Not everyone needs my attention and knowledge.

CUSTOMER RELATIONSHIP MANAGEMENT

The right team won't work for the wrong person. I must be an expert planner in my craft and lead with organized direction.

COURAGE

Doing anything alone can be nerve wracking. Not impossible. Courageously support and encourage your own will and spring into action with dedicated efforts.

EVERYTHING COSTS

Save more or learn to make more
money.

NO LACKING

Time waits for nobody, so I won't wait idly. I value my time and effort in everything and everyone.

AMBITION

I'm much closer to my dreams than I can imagine. Most of the time it just takes positive thinking. Other times it takes less thinking and more action. I will remain compassionate no matter who decides to stay or leave.

SACRIFICE

Never complain about what you must do when you hear what you should do. Just acknowledge and adjust accordingly.

ENTREPRENEUR'S DUTY

I sell the process, the shortcuts, the journey, the trials, the failures, the losses, the hard work, and the smart work I have knowledge of to accomplish a task.

LET GO

Learning to cut ties consistently is a skill to master when aiming for progression. There's no malice in God's time. Trust the process as divine.

MOVE ALREADY

My action is my influence. I must not be lazy in my faith, judgment, and action!

ALWAYS TWO SIDES

I smile in the face of disappointment because I know that it could have been far worse. I pray to never lose my gratitude or faith.

NOT FORCING NOTHING

Forget going where I am allowed. I'm only interested in going where I'm invited or requested. It's nothing personal.

LUCK

Tomorrow is another day. One day, however, I won't be as lucky to see it.

WHAT'S OK?

Money isn't everything, and love doesn't pay the bills. Think, build, and respond rationally.

SIMPLE 'L' RULE

When learning anything new or old in this world, remember to act and detach from the Losses you take along the way. That's how you earn your living.

GET UP

I could be good and still lose because I'm not good enough. I must be good a few times over to be great in the eyes of others. It's great already that I am willing to push, no matter how many times I must get myself back up. I'm going after it until I master it and then some!

TEN TOES

Always reassess, readjust, and recommit to all that you have the best intentions for. It's okay to be emotionally ignorant. However, it's not okay to remain unaware. Be pure in your accountability and control the narrative.

NO SHADE

Perspective and preference — that is all that makes us different. Sharing these things with one another gives us the opportunity to grow a better understanding of community development.

TIME AND MONEY

When delegating becomes overextending, quickly change course of action, or adapt and improve on the current skill(s) necessary. Don't wait to feel defeated about something out of your control.

STANDING ON PURPOSE

I'm in love with my purpose, and I'm open to whoever complements that on a journey of their own.

CREATING OPTIONS

A good teacher can't teach every student, but a great teacher can teach one lesson multiple ways.

BE RESPONSIBLE

Be the plug you seek if you refuse to
bend. In the process, become the source
that all plugs turn to for light and love.

INDEPENDENT
THINKER

The people with the most opinions about
me aren't doing better than me. I won't
compare myself unnecessarily.

CONTROL THE NARRATIVE

Don't get distracted by a path that you didn't choose intentionally. Change directions at any point and continue to grow where you feel you can learn.

BRAVE HEART

One loss doesn't mean game over. You only lose when you stop trying to win. So have the heart to fail and get back to putting in the work necessary.

COMPREHENDING

Just because I don't see it well in this moment doesn't mean I'm not listening. I'll take my time digesting and reflecting on new information until I comprehend.

CALM FOR A REASON

I don't get riled up about anything I'm not passionate about. What's for me will be. I have that much faith.

WORKOUT

Mentally, physically, and spiritually, I'm getting strong for when life comes at me fast or slow.

RISK MANAGEMENT

Desire should never out-balance
priorities in life. Better time
management prevents losses.

LOOK UP

In the process of empowering myself, I can't belittle myself.

COMMITED

I choose this because I want this, and I intend to make the best out of the commitment.

COACHING STARS

Suggestions that improve the self and the ecosystem at large should always be acknowledged and rewarded with fair trade.

HAVING STANDARDS

I can't ignore my standards. I only pay for disappointment when I do.

SELF-DEVELOPMENT

No situation is permanent. With the courage to change, I plan to do so.

NEVER LOSE

If I learned from the experience, I didn't lose.

BELIEF SYSTEM

I can achieve the best version of myself. No matter how challenging it may be on the road to self-development, I'm in charge of my own discipline. The end of my journey stops at my last breath.

MOVING WITH PURPOSE

I'm striving to become better than I was yesterday every single day because the journey of longevity isn't a rush.

CHECK YOURSELF

How can I be more just and righteous without being passive-aggressive?

GENERAL PRINCIPLE

Don't send for me when you can call me directly.

PEACEFULLY SPEAKING

Sometimes I'm just saying how I feel. It's not personal, and I won't hurry to explain myself all the time. Let it be just that. Stoic and calm.

GREAT MANIFESTO

I say my ideas out loud because I believe I'll manifest the assistance I need to make things happen along the way. I am mindful of my own actions or inaction, and I make no excuses.

A GOOD MEMORY

I pray to always remember and acknowledge what and who I have in my corner. I can't make the mistake of letting value go over my head.

DON'T SLIP

Every decision must be accounted for. I'm not living idly with my ideals. I'm standing in my purpose, I'm planning, and I'm organizing my direction.

THE MATRIX

I am a walking advertisement. In the process of learning to monetize my purpose and value in the marketplace, I am controlling my narrative.

KNOW YOUR LANE

I believe the world has its story set already. Minding my business is deciding not to take things personally. We are all living through our own perspectives. I feel lucky when I can adapt my views and get along with those who share them... When it's not for me, I'll remove myself. It's nothing personal.

BROKEN MIRRORS

Know yourself before you look in the mirror, because there are days when you will look in the mirror with scars and bruises. Don't get rattled. Time heals all things.

REFOCUS

I let something disrupt my energy. Now that I've acknowledged it, I'll let it go and breathe freely again. I've seen this before. I'm still here with purpose.

YOU'RE NOT ALONE

There are people like you out there. It's your job to self-identify and be accountable to realize and value others like you.

COMPASSION

Don't judge your kindness. Just be kind.

PERSONAL VOW

I strive to never let go of a good thing and to protect myself from anything that will devalue my worth.

IT'S NOT JUST YOU

Perspective can change my life. It can also help me become a better friend.

KEEP UP

I won't get far if I don't trust myself. Prepared or not, there are others who are choosing to just go for it. I won't get left behind in constant contemplation.

ON ME

If I got it, you got it. If you got it, I got it. If you don't have it and I got it, you got it. If I don't have it and you do, I got it. And if we both don't have it, let's talk about how we can get it. Especially if it's family. If it's me at the head of the family, I'll speak to someone with whom I choose to share my legacy. Family.

CAREFUL TRUSTING

Everything is forgivable until you lose one's gratitude.

MOVING FORWARD

We only forgive when we love or can gain
from the offender.

SELF-MAINTENANCE

I am not a product of my circumstances. I can develop into a greater version of myself. There's value in discipline.

GOD'S POWER

What I can handle and what I can manifest is all from God. I am his patron.

REMAIN CONSISTENT

Be proud. Remain proud. Be grateful. Remain grateful. It's okay to forgive yourself and keep learning.

FAIR TRADE

If I can't be convinced, I won't commit. I won't compromise myself for the benefit of other parties. Nor will I overextend. If my time and effort for my skills can't be compensated with fair trade, I'll remain focused on personal matters and projects that I believe will benefit me.

FULFILLMENT MATTERS

Building a team isn't about shortening responsibilities. It's about executing projects and goals with trust and direction so that everyone on the team can contribute and finish feeling fulfilled and accomplished.

STOP OVEREXTENDING

I give in spaces where I can ask genuinely. Where I can't ask for anything, I do my best to give willingly and let go completely to avoid harboring ill will or remaining stuck in the past.

GENUINE PILLARS

Consistency. Commitment. Comfort. Caution. Curiosity. Communication. Comprehension. You'll need everyone of them to make anything worth while work.

PEACE BE ONTO YOU

Some must go through darkness to become a light for others.

GOOD SPEAKER

The hardest part of public speaking is
finding those willing to listen to you.
Be capable of relaying a message that
listeners can receive and take value from
without pity or force.

CHOOSING LONGEVITY

They'll keep me at arm's length while waiting for me to evolve and become. I'll return that energy with distance, development, and success. Let karma be the best form of payment to family, friends, and community.

DREAM

I'm willing to fail early into lessons that'll help me become successful. I will accomplish all that I aspire and then some.

"WHY?" MATTERS

There's no point in entertaining conversations from a position of need. I must figure out my own "why?" first, then grab the large end of the stick with confidence.

NOT FOR NOTHING

I'm not working overtime to my detriment.

FLOW STATE

Even when I am moving fast, I am still walking slow. It's never any pressure.

THIS IS REAL

What I could've done won't change what really happened. Adjust. Sometimes that's the toughest part of development. Recognizing when my pride and ego are getting the best of me is what will truly make me a great leader.

REAL GRATITUDE

What is not okay will be. I have that much faith in what I have and what I will make.

CHARISMA

I don't want to be different. I just want to be happy. There's a real thrill and simplicity in that.

MOVE ALONG

How can I be mad when the sun is shining on me?

IT'S OK

There's room to breathe freely outside of my box and community.

CHARGE UP

Someone must make the decision. When you're put in position to lead, be clear and have faith in yourself. To be a leader is to prepare and present the best option with certainty for others to follow.

ALWAYS PRAYING

Forcing anything in this world will only give me heartache. I choose to let go and pray on the things that I truly wish to manifest.

FACTORS OF GROWTH

If I can teach and promote what I
do, I can make a profit. I must be
steadfast in all my customer relationship
management.

DETACH

I detach from anything, anyone, and any place that does not put me in a position to win. I want to win! I'm intentional.

ECOSYSTEM

Never disregard the importance of community development. Never neglect the responsibilities of family language and chemistry.

OPEN CHALLENGE

It's my job to make it easier for my patrons to support me. I accept that challenge.

MERCH

I'm building a business, not just freelancing.

CONFIDENCE

Speak like you know what money looks like on and within you. If that offends anyone, let it.

BE

Stop becoming and be who you are. Don't let preparation prevent you from action.

DON'T BE SALTY

Salt is seasoning too! I accept every grain because I know too many who are just salty.

SAME COIN

On the other side of love is criticism. You must manage your pride and ego. Learn to value the two sides of the same coin.

THE RIGHT CROWD

Successful people strive with one another. I'm finding my lane with lessons from the past because I refuse to get left behind.

CHEERS!

Raise a glass to the lessons learned and the wisdom still to come. It's enough to celebrate life.

THE LIFE CHOSEN

I'm supporting myself while supporting my business in hopes to one day create and support my family. That is why and how I continue to take the risk of entrepreneurship.

ACKNOWLEDGEMENTS

Glory be to God for providing me with the strength, wisdom, and ability to complete this book and deliver its message, mission, and purpose. I am grateful to my dad for being an excellent role model for community leadership, my mom, Karen Tapper, for supporting me during the moments when I couldn't do it myself, and my sister, Firdows Liameed, for being proud of me even during my darkest moments. To all those who supported me, encouraged me, and embraced my views, thank you for being my patron and reading my mantras.

Lastly, I dedicate this book to my children, if I am fortunate enough to raise any. This compilation of letters that I've written since I was seventeen years old is for passing on as much wisdom as I can muster into your future legacy and progress. I hope that you will cherish these words, affirmations, and mantras for generations to come.

Dear children,

When you love, prepare yourself to forgive someone who may never understand how they have wronged you. Learn yourself, your core values, and your principles. Accept love as a luxury, along with the mistakes that come with it. Be kind to yourself, and never tolerate that which you're willing to forgive. Happiness is attainable to everyone, especially you!

Remember that your praise must always be louder than your criticism, and your apology must always be louder than your disrespect. No matter what happens in life, good or bad, be direct in your actions and accountable for the results. That is what it means to be just. That is what my father is. That is how I hope to be. By God's will, that is how I hope for you to be as well. Can you say amen?

I will always be there for you in love, liberty, and spirit. But you must learn these things well for yourself. The patience of a man has no tolerance for those without a code of ethics, without principles. Morally stand up for yourself. Study the pride and elegance of your family. Be just with others and never abandon the trust and communication with family. Family is truly all you got. Respect and fight for your name, because like my father, I took my time in naming you. Build up your home and stand ten toes down on what you believe and desire to achieve. You are most capable.

ABOUT AUTHOR

Gafar "Wale Abdul" Liameed, also known as the Gentle Spokesperson, is a visionary entrepreneur who has dedicated his career to turning ideas and documented moments into lasting memories. He is the founder and owner of Royalviewz Worthy Group LLC, a prominent branding and marketing agency that collaborates with creative professionals to enhance their reach and engagement across all digital and social platforms.

Originally from Brooklyn and raised in the United States and Nigeria, Gafar settled in Chicago in 2015 and has since worked as a brand strategist, media producer, customer relationship manager, and consultant. He has provided media marketing solutions for artists, models, and businesses, including Stack or Starve, Bikettle, and GQ Gentlemen.

Gafar's commitment to excellence and attention to detail have made him a sought-after expert in his field. He continued to hone his entrepreneurial skills and built a successful business in the photography and videography industry. His passion for capturing life's most precious moments has inspired him to author his first book, "Affirmations for Entrepreneurs: Daily Mantras for Life, Love, and Liberty."

This devotional guide and reference book is a collection of affirmations that have helped Gafar overcome challenges and achieve success in his own entrepreneurial journey.

As an entrepreneur with a third-world perspective, Gafar pushes the boundaries with the dream of liberating the idea of the starving artist with economic trade and education. He focuses his passion and purpose on building and establishing a haven for his community through arts and business development. He strives to connect people with their goals and dreams and be a living example of what's possible through courage, creativity, accountability, and relentless work ethic.

Affirmations for Entrepreneurs: Daily

Mantras for Life, Love, and Liberty is Gafar's debut book, and he is continuously seeking ways to improve his writing and engage with readers. He would be immensely grateful if you could leave a review on Amazon if you enjoyed his book, as it would mean the world to him and help him grow as an author. Thank you for your support.

Jeanette will never forget, the best birthday party she has ever had.

www.ingramcontent.com/pod-product-compliance
Lightning Source LLC
LaVergne TN
LVHW051248080426
835513LV00016B/1813